HANDS-ON
Science

Electricity and Magnets

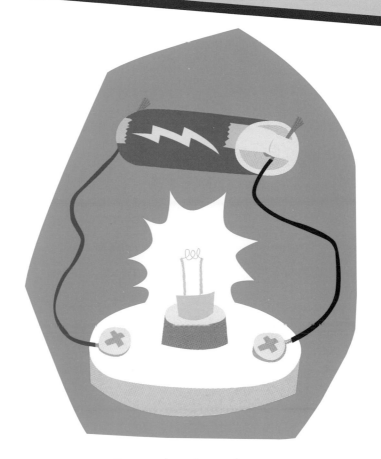

Sarah Angliss

Illustrated by David Le Jars

KINGFISHER

NEW YORK

KINGFISHER
Larousse Kingfisher Chambers Inc.
80 Maiden Lane
New York, New York 10038
www.kingfisherpub.com

Produced for Kingfisher by PAGE*One*

First published in 2001
10 9 8 7 6 5 4 3 2

2TR/1101/TWP/GRST/150SMA

LIBRARY OF CONGRESS CATALOGING-IN-PUBLICATION DATA
Angliss, Sarah.
    Electricity and magnets / by Sarah Angliss.
        p. cm.— (Hands on science)
    Includes index.
    ISBN 0-7534-5349-5
    1. Electricity—Experiments—Juvenile literature.
    2. Magnetism—Experiments—Juvenile literature.
    [1. Electricity—Experiments. 2. Magnetism—Experiments.
    3. Experiments.] I. Title. II. Hands on science (Kingfisher)

QC527.2 .A54 2001
537—dc21   00-048140

Printed in Singapore

For PAGEOne
Creative Director Bob Gordon
Project Editor Miriam Richardson
Designers Monica Bratt, Tim Stansfield

For Kingfisher
Managing Editor Clive Wilson
Coordinating Editor Laura Marshall
Production Manager Oonagh Phelan
DTP Coordinator Nicky Studdart

CONTENTS

Getting started

Every time you turn on a light or watch TV, you are using electricity. When you close the refrigerator door or play a tape, you use magnetism. If you've ever wanted to know what electricity and magnetism are, how they work, and how they are used, then this is the book for you. It is packed with activities to try and things to make. Before you start, read these pages carefully—they give you a lot of useful advice.

Are you well connected?

If you try the electrical activities on pages 10–37, you'll find that electricity only flows between things that are stuck together properly. So when you build a circuit, make sure it has really good connections.

Ask an adult to strip the plastic off of the ends of plastic-coated wires. Electricity can only flow through the bare metal—it does not flow through plastic.

Attach a wire to the terminals of a battery with tape or modeling clay. Make sure the metal part of the wire touches the metal part of the battery.

The right stuff

Most of the activities and games in this book use everyday things like batteries, spoons, lemons, and paper clips. Sometimes you'll need more unusual items, like iron filings, steel wool, and small light bulbs. Try your local toy or hobby store for these.

Small light bulbs that screw into a base like this are the easiest kind to use, but you can also use bulbs without a base.

For most of the activities, any small battery will do. Put it in a radio to make sure it works.

You will also need several lengths of plastic-coated (insulated) wire.

Try to get two straight bar magnets like these.

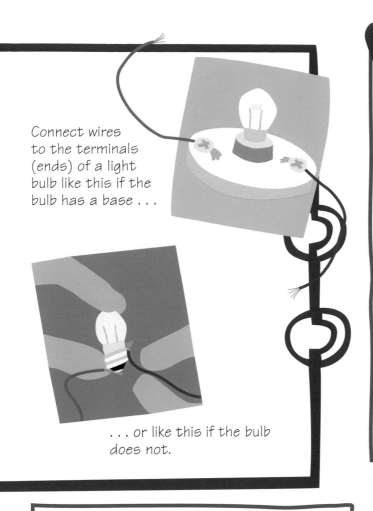

Connect wires to the terminals (ends) of a light bulb like this if the bulb has a base . . .

. . . or like this if the bulb does not.

Warning

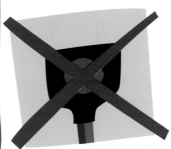

Safety first! The electrical activities in this book use small batteries that give off very little electricity.

Never experiment with electricity that comes out of plugs and sockets at home or school. It is thousands of times more powerful than a small battery. It can kill.

Never play near overhead pylons or electricity substations. Even when you are not touching them, electricity can jump from them and kill you.

Stuck for words?

If you come across a word you don't understand or you just want to find out more, take a look at the glossary on pages 38 and 39.

Having problems?

If something doesn't work at first, don't give up.

Look through the instructions and illustrations again to see if there's anything you have missed.

Clock symbol

The clock symbol at the beginning of each experiment shows you how many minutes the activity should take. All of the experiments take between 5 and 30 minutes. If you are using glue, allow extra time for drying.

Even the greatest scientists sometimes had problems with their experiments. Take J. J. Thompson, for example, the scientist who discovered the electron. He was so clumsy, his students wouldn't let him go near his own equipment!

What a tingle!

Electricity is a form of energy—it makes things happen. It can heat up a toaster or light up a bulb. We usually think of electricity as flowing through wires, but static electricity doesn't flow at all. You can make static electricity by rubbing certain materials together. This rubs invisible particles called electrons off of one thing and onto the other, giving each of them a charge. The thing that loses electrons has an opposite charge to the one that has gained them.

Snake charmer

Use static electricity to move things without using your hands! Make sure all your materials are dry.

YOU WILL NEED
10
- TISSUE PAPER
- A PLASTIC RULER
- A SCRAP OF NYLON FABRIC
- SCISSORS

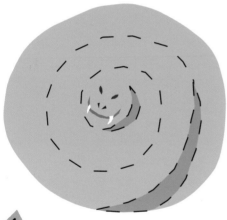

1 Copy this pattern onto the tissue paper and cut it out. Cut along the dotted line, then hold one end to make a spiraling snake. Make more snakes to go with it.

2 Rub a plastic ruler several times with a scrap of nylon.

3 Wave the ruler close to your snakes. Can you lift them up without touching them?

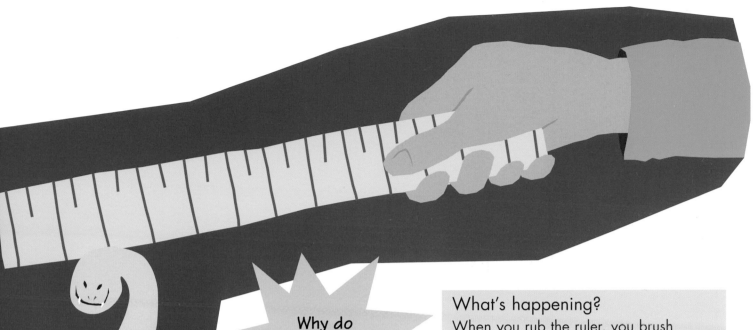

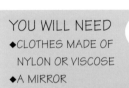

Why do the snakes dance?

What's happening?
When you rub the ruler, you brush tiny particles called electrons off of the nylon and onto the plastic. This makes static electricity. The tissue paper is slightly short of electrons. When the ruler is close enough, the paper moves toward the ruler so it can "grab" the extra electrons.

Fashion victim
Listen carefully while you take off some nylon or viscose clothes. If it's dark, look into a mirror while you do this. Do you hear tiny crackles or see tiny sparks?

YOU WILL NEED

5

◆CLOTHES MADE OF NYLON OR VISCOSE
◆A MIRROR

What's happening?
The crackles you hear and the sparks you see when you take off the clothes are caused by electrons moving between your body and your clothes. They are just like mini thunder and lightning!

STORMY WEATHER
If enough charge builds up in a cloud, it may release itself suddenly in a bolt of lightning. The heat of the lightning makes the air expand, creating a clap of thunder.

Make it move

An object tends not to keep its charge. If possible, it will dump it onto other things nearby. You can use this fact to make things move. Objects pull toward each other, or attract, if they have opposite charges. This pulls them close enough to share electrons and get rid of their charges. If two objects have the same charge, they can't dump electrons onto each other, and they push each other apart, or repel.

What makes the butterfly's wings move?

It's alive!

Charge up a delicate paper butterfly to bring it to life.

YOU WILL NEED
- ◆ A METAL PAPER CLIP
- ◆ AN EMPTY JAR
- ◆ MODELING CLAY
- ◆ ALUMINUM FOIL
- ◆ TISSUE PAPER
- ◆ A PLASTIC RULER
- ◆ A SCRAP OF NYLON FABRIC
- ◆ SCISSORS

20

1 Uncurl your paper clip, then bend it into the shape shown in the picture.

2 Take a piece of aluminum foil, about the size of the palm of your hand, and roll it into a tight ball. Poke the end of your paper clip into the ball of foil.

3 Rest your paper clip on the rim of the jar, using a piece of modeling clay to keep it in place. Cut a tiny butterfly out of tissue paper. Lay it on your paper clip, inside the jar.

4 Rub the plastic ruler with a scrap of nylon. This will give it a charge (see pages 6–7). Watch the butterfly carefully as you bring the ruler very close to the foil ball. Can you see the butterfly's wings moving?

What's happening?

The charged ruler has a lot of extra electrons that it wants to dump onto other objects around it. It can do this when you bring it close to the ball. Electrons move through metal easily, so they flow through the foil and the paper clip and into the paper. Both paper wings get the same charge, so they repel each other and open up.

In the bag

Cut a strip from the bag and rub it with the nylon. This will give the strip a charge by giving it extra electrons. Then rub the other objects with the nylon and bring them close to the charged plastic strip. If an object has lost electrons, it will have an opposite charge to the strip, so it will be attracted toward the strip. If it has gained electrons, it will have the same charge as the strip, so the two will repel each other.

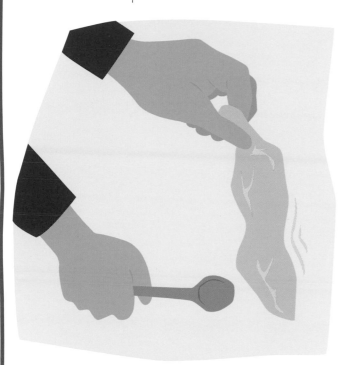

What's happening?

When you rub plastic objects, such as the ballpoint pen casing, they gain electrons. That's why they repel the strip. Metal objects, like the fork, lose electrons, so they attract the strip. A few objects, including the eraser, have little effect on the strip, because they hardly pick up any charge at all.

Hair-raising

This experiment works best on a dry day. Run the plastic comb through your hair over and over. Do it as fast as you can without pulling your hair. Stop after half a minute or so. What happens? (You can also try rubbing your hair with a balloon—it has the same effect.)

What's happening?

The comb brushes electrons onto your hair, giving each of your hairs the same type of charge. The hairs can't dump their extra charge, so they repel each other, making them stand on end.

DISASTER IN THE AIR
In May 1937, the huge airship *Hindenburg* went up in flames when the crew threw some ropes to the ground. They didn't realize that stormy weather had built up a lot of charge on the ship's outer shell. This charge flowed along the ropes and into the ground, causing a spark that set the gas inside the airship alight.

Wire it up

So far, you've only experimented with static electricity—the kind that's made when you brush electrons onto things or rub electrons off of them. However, there's another very useful kind of electricity that's made by moving electrons. It's called current electricity. Electrons can easily move through metal. Using a battery, you can push them all the way through a metal wire. To do this, you need to make the wire into a complete loop, called a circuit, that lets them flow out of the battery and back in again.

Bright idea

When current electricity flows through this circuit, it lights up a bulb.

YOU WILL NEED ▶ 10
- ◆ A SMALL FLASHLIGHT BULB WITH A MAXIMUM VOLTAGE OF 4.5 VOLTS
- ◆ A 1.5-VOLT AA BATTERY
- ◆ TWO INSULATED WIRES
- ◆ TAPE

1 Ask an adult to strip about ¾ in. (2cm) of plastic from each end of the wires.

2 Tape the bare end of one wire to the silver knob on the top of the battery. This knob is called the positive terminal.

3 Tape the bare end of the other wire to the silver base of the battery. This is called the negative terminal.

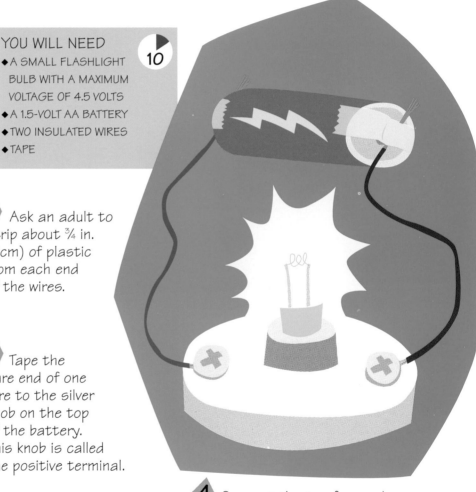

4 Connect the two free ends of wire to the light bulb. Does your bulb glow?

What's happening?
You have a made a complete circuit. Electrons can flow out of the battery, through one wire, through the bulb, through the other wire, then into the battery again. When they flow through the bulb, they make it glow.

Bridge the gap

Follow the steps in "Bright idea" (left) to make a light bulb glow. Ask an adult to cut one of the wires in half to break the circuit. Keep everything else in place. Ask your adult helper to strip the two free ends of broken wire, then touch both free ends of bare wire with a metal paper clip at the same time. What happens to the bulb?

What happens to the bulb when you break the circuit?

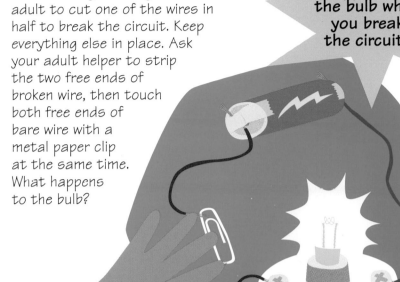

YOU WILL NEED

◆ A SMALL FLASHLIGHT BULB WITH A MAXIMUM VOLTAGE OF 4.5 VOLTS
◆ A 1.5-VOLT AA BATTERY
◆ TWO INSULATED WIRES
◆ A METAL PAPER CLIP
◆ TAPE

What's happening?

When you break the circuit, electricity can't flow all the way around it, so the bulb stops glowing. The metal paper clip can bridge the gap in the broken circuit. When you press it against the two bare ends of broken wire, electricity can flow through it, from one piece of wire to the other. The paper clip completes the circuit, letting the bulb glow. In this way, it works as a switch.

FLASHBACK

Say it with lights

Electricity came into homes in the late 1800s. At that time, it was an expensive luxury seen only in the richest city homes. Electric light was so costly that people only put it in their most important rooms. Some people who could afford just one light bulb decided to put it in the hall. They left their electric light on all day—even when they were out—to show it off to passersby.

PINBALL WIZARD

The steel ball in this pinball machine bridges the gap between the target and the base of the machine. This completes a circuit that makes lights glow and buzzers buzz. The circuit switches on and off in an instant as the ball moves around, adding to the excitement of the game.

Thick and thin

Electricity can flow through any metal wires in a circuit, but it flows more easily through thick wires than thin ones. The amount of electricity flowing through a wire is called the current. If you use a thinner wire, it is harder for the battery to push electricity through it, so it will produce a smaller current.

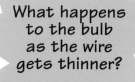

What happens to the bulb as the wire gets thinner?

Dim the light

See what happens to your bulb when you use a thin wire in this circuit.

YOU WILL NEED
15
- A SMALL FLASHLIGHT BULB WITH A MAXIMUM VOLTAGE OF 4.5 VOLTS
- A 1.5-VOLT AA BATTERY
- TWO INSULATED WIRES
- A PIECE OF STEEL WOOL
- TAPE

1 Following the steps in "Bridge the gap" (page 11), build a circuit that uses a paper clip switch to light up a bulb.

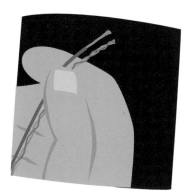

2 Pull and twist some steel wool into a strand about 2 ¼ in. (5.75cm) long. Make the strand about as thick as your insulated wires.

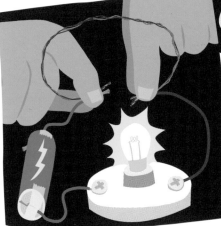

3 Use the steel wool strand, instead of a paper clip, to bridge the gap in your circuit. Make sure the bulb glows.

4 Take away about three fourths of the steel wool and make a strand that's just as long, but much thinner. Use it to bridge the gap again. How does your bulb look now?

5 Make the strand even thinner. How does this affect the bulb?

What's happening?
It is hard for electricity to flow through a circuit that contains a thin strand of steel wool. The battery can only make a small current in a circuit like this. Little electricity reaches the bulb, so it glows dimly. When you use an even thinner strand, the battery makes an even smaller current, so the bulb glows even more dimly.

Shortcut

The wires in this experiment could get warm—ask an adult to help. Follow the steps in "Bright idea" (page 10) to build a circuit that makes a bulb glow. Ask an adult to strip the ends of an extra wire. Then touch the bare ends of this wire against the terminals of your battery. Make sure you touch both terminals at once. What happens to the bulb?

YOU WILL NEED

15

◆ A SMALL FLASHLIGHT BULB WITH A MAXIMUM VOLTAGE OF 3 VOLTS OR 4.5 VOLTS
◆ A 1.5-VOLT AA BATTERY
◆ THREE INSULATED WIRES

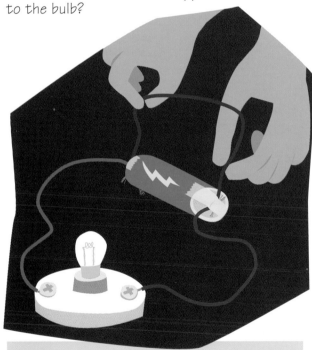

What's happening?

When you put the extra wire across the terminals of your battery, the bulb goes out. Electricity flows through your extra wire, completely bypassing the bulb. If you look closely at your light bulb, you can see why. Inside the bulb is a thin coil of metal, called a filament, that carries electricity. Your extra wire is much thicker than this filament, so electricity flows through it far more easily. Your extra wire is a short circuit—an easier route for the electric current to take.

Getting warmer

Try "Dim the light" (far left) again, using only two thin strands of steel wool. Leave the bulb glowing very dimly for at least a minute, then feel the steel wool. What do you notice?

What's happening?

Because it is very hard for electricity to flow through a very thin strand of steel wool, it turns into a different form of energy—heat. The heat makes the steel wool feel slightly warmer to the touch.

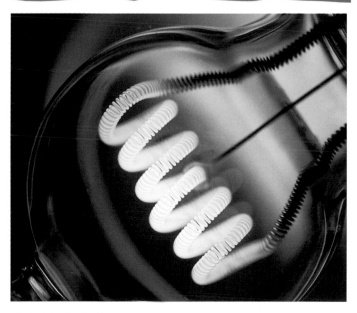

WARM GLOW
A light bulb can turn electricity into light because it contains a very thin filament. It is hard for the electricity to flow through the filament, so the energy turns into heat, which makes the filament glow white hot. This is how the bulb makes light.

Go with the flow

Electricity can flow through some substances more easily than others. It can flow very easily through substances called conductors. Metal and water are good conductors. An insulator is a substance that makes it practically impossible for electricity to flow. Plastics are usually good insulators.

The right stuff?

Here's a handy way to tell if some everyday items are conductors or insulators.

YOU WILL NEED

- A SMALL FLASHLIGHT BULB WITH A MAXIMUM VOLTAGE OF 4.5 VOLTS
- A 1.5-VOLT AA BATTERY
- TWO INSULATED WIRES
- A METAL PAPER CLIP
- TAPE
- OBJECTS MADE OF DIFFERENT MATERIALS, LIKE AN ERASER, A COIN, A WOODEN SPOON, A GLASS CUP, A SHEET OF PAPER, A PLASTIC BALLPOINT PEN, AND A CERAMIC CUP.

15

1 Follow the steps in "Bridge the gap" (page 11) to make a circuit with a break in it. Make sure the bulb glows when you bridge the break with a paper clip.

What's happening?

The bulb glows when you put some objects, such as a metal coin, in the circuit. This is because these objects are conductors. It does not glow when you put other objects, such as the pencil eraser, in the circuit. This is because they are insulators. Conductors, unlike insulators, are made of materials that readily let electrons flow through them. This why they let current flow so easily.

2 Replace the paper clip with another object, like a wooden spoon. Does the bulb glow now? Repeat with each of your other objects in turn. Which ones make the bulb glow? Which ones don't?

Water and air

You can test two very special substances—water and air—to see whether they conduct electricity. To test water, dip the two wires into a small saucer of water. To test air, simply hold the two wires up in the air.

10

YOU WILL NEED
- A SMALL FLASHLIGHT BULB WITH A MAXIMUM VOLTAGE OF 4.5 VOLTS
- A 1.5-VOLT AA BATTERY
- TWO INSULATED WIRES
- TAPE
- A SAUCER OF WATER

Does water conduct electricity? Does air?

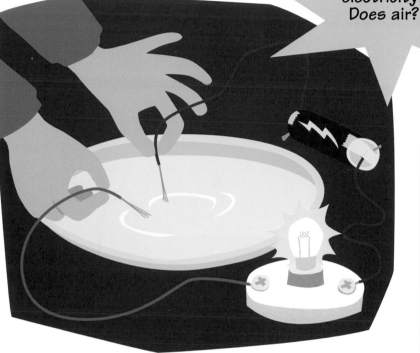

What's happening?

The bulb glows when you bridge the gap in the circuit with water, but not when you bridge it with air. Water, like metal, allows electricity to flow through it—it's a conductor. Air, on the other hand, is an insulator. But sometimes, when it is far more powerful, electricity can flow through air. Lightning, for example, is electricity that is flowing through the air. You can make enough harmless static electricity to jump a short distance through the air in "It's alive!" (page 8).

BIRDS ON A WIRE

There is enough current running through this wire to kill. Birds can sit on it safely, though, because almost all of the current flows through the wire, not the birds. This is because the wire is a much better conductor of electricity than the birds. Never try this yourself. If you reach out to a bare wire, electricity could flow through the wire, through your body, and into the ground, which could kill you.

Powerhouse

A battery is a mini electricity generator. When a battery is in a circuit, it gradually releases the electrical energy stored inside it. This energy pushes a stream of electrons around the circuit, making an electric current. You can make your own electricity generator, just like a battery, from a few coins and some supplies from the kitchen.

Animal electricity

Frogs' legs were used to make the first battery. In a very gory experiment in 1791, scientist Luigi Galvani noticed that the legs of dead frogs twitched when he touched them with two different metals. Another scientist, Alessandro Volta, used this discovery to make a battery from metal disks soaked in salty water.

Fruity tingle

Make enough electricity from a lemon to feel a tingle on your tongue!

YOU WILL NEED
5
◆ TWO COINS MADE OF DIFFERENT METALS
◆ A LEMON
◆ TWO INSULATED WIRES
◆ A SHARP KNIFE (ASK AN ADULT)

1 Ask an adult to cut two small slits in the lemon with the sharp knife. The slits should be about 1 in. (2.5cm) apart and long enough to hold your coins.

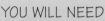
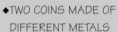

2 Now ask the adult to strip about ¾ in. (2cm) off the ends of your insulated wires. Push a bare end of one wire into each slit. Push a coin into each slit to hold the wires in place.

3 Put the loose end of each wire on your tongue, making sure the wires don't touch. Can you feel anything?

Change the recipe

Lemons aren't the only fruit that will make electricity. Try "Fruity tingle" (left) again with other types of fruits and vegetables. Change your metal coins, too. If you run out of different coins to try, use nails instead. Which homemade battery makes the biggest tingle?

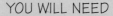
YOU WILL NEED
- COINS AND NAILS MADE OF VARIOUS METALS
- DIFFERENT FRUITS AND VEGETABLES
- INSULATED WIRES

What fruits and vegetables make the best batteries?

What's happening?

Many combinations of fruits or vegetables and metal will work as mini batteries. You need to use a food that is acidic (potatoes and pineapples are good), along with two different metals. Some combinations produce a much bigger tingle than others.

4 Pull one wire out of the lemon, then repeat step 3. What do you feel now?

What's happening?

The lemon and the coins make a simple battery. They can't produce enough electricity to power a light bulb, but they should make enough for you to feel a tingle on your tongue. If you pull out one wire, you break the circuit, so you don't feel the tingle anymore. Inside a real battery, there are two plates made of different metals, just like the coins. They are separated by a type of chemical called an acid, like the juice of the lemon.

A LIFEJACKET
As soon as this sailor falls into the sea, the salt water fills a hollow salt-water battery on his lifejacket. This activates the battery, which powers an emergency light that can be seen by rescue teams.

The big push

A battery has to push electricity all the way around a circuit. If the circuit has a lot of parts that make it difficult for electricity to flow, the battery will make a very small current. This would happen, for instance, if the circuit contained a lot of skinny wires. To produce more current in the same circuit, you would need to use a battery that can give electrons a bigger push. The electrical "push" of a battery is measured in volts. A 9-volt battery, for example, has six times the push of a 1.5-volt battery.

Does a 9-volt battery make the bulbs any brighter?

Party lights

See what happens when a battery has to push current through more than one bulb.

YOU WILL NEED
- A 1.5-VOLT AA BATTERY
- A 9-VOLT BATTERY
- UP TO FIVE SMALL FLASHLIGHT BULBS, EACH WITH A MAXIMUM VOLTAGE OF 4.5 VOLTS
- UP TO SIX WIRES
- TAPE

15

1 Follow the steps in "Bright idea" (page 10) to make a bulb glow. Try to remember how bright the bulb is.

2 Add another bulb to the circuit, like this. Do both bulbs glow? How bright are they?

3 Add more light bulbs to the circuit. What happens to their brightness? Do they always glow?

4 When you have three or more bulbs in the circuit, swap your battery for a 9-volt one and see what happens.

What's happening?

As you add more bulbs to this circuit, each one gets dimmer. That's because the bulbs have to share the battery's voltage. The battery has to use some of its voltage to push electricity through each bulb. The current in the circuit reduces every time a bulb is added. If enough bulbs are added, the current becomes so low that it can't make the bulbs glow at all. A 9-volt battery pushes more current around the circuit, so it can make more bulbs glow.

Dimmer switch

Follow the steps in "Bridge the gap" (page 11) to make a broken circuit. Bridge the gap in the circuit with a soft mechanical pencil lead. Does the bulb glow?

What happens if you vary the length of the lead between the wires?

What's happening?

As you vary the length of pencil lead between the wires, you change the brightness of the bulb. That's because it is hard for electricity to flow through the lead. The longer the lead is, the more voltage the battery needs to push electricity through it. This leaves less voltage to make the bulb glow.

String them along

Follow steps 1 and 2 of "Party lights" (left) to light up two bulbs. Now replace the wires with very long ones. Does this change the brightness of the bulbs?

What's happening?

When you make the wires in your circuit longer, the brightness of the bulbs hardly changes at all. That's because electricity flows easily through the wires. No matter how long the wires are, very little of the battery's voltage is used to push electricity through them.

ELECTRIC GUITAR

The volume knob on this electric guitar works like your dimmer switch. When the knob is turned, two wires move nearer or farther apart along a piece of graphite (the material used for pencil lead). This varies the voltage that is available for the amplifier and loudspeaker. When they get more voltage, they make a louder sound.

Neat work

Circuits don't have to be thick and bulky. In fact, you can make a circuit that has wires as thin as a sheet of paper.

A circuit like this can be squeezed into the tightest of spaces—for example, inside a personal stereo or a computer.

Circuit board

Using aluminum foil, you can make a flat circuit that you can turn into an exciting picture!

YOU WILL NEED
20
- A SHEET OF ALUMINUM FOIL
- A STIFF PIECE OF CARDBOARD ABOUT 6 IN. (15CM) BY 8 IN. (20CM)
- A 9-VOLT BATTERY
- TWO SMALL FLASHLIGHT BULBS WITH A MAXIMUM VOLTAGE OF 4.5 VOLTS
- GLUE AND TAPE
- SHORT INSULATED WIRES
- SCISSORS

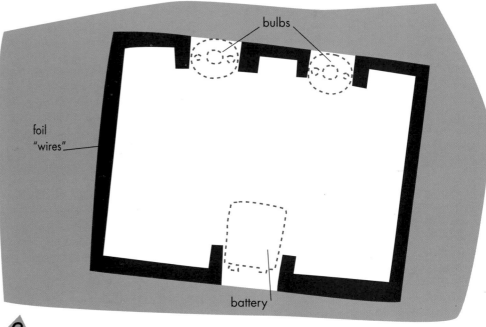

bulbs

foil "wires"

battery

1 Cut out some neat strips of aluminum foil about ¾ in. (2cm) wide and 6 in. (15cm) long.

2 Draw this pattern onto the piece of cardboard. This is the design for your circuit.

What conducts the electricity in your circuit board?

3 Glue strips of foil over the parts of the design that are wires.

Glowing masterpiece

Make two holes in the sheet of paper so that when you place it on your circuit, the light bulbs will poke through. Design a colorful picture that will make use of your bulbs, then stick it onto your circuit. Keep the bulbs in place with some modeling clay. When you're finished, stand back and admire your glowing masterpiece!

YOU WILL NEED
20
- THE CIRCUIT YOU MADE IN "CIRCUIT BOARD" (LEFT)
- MODELING CLAY
- A THICK SHEET OF PLAIN PAPER ABOUT 6 IN. (15CM) BY 8 IN. (20CM)
- TWO LONG WIRES
- A CRAFT KNIFE (ASK AN ADULT)
- CRAYONS, PAINTS, OR FELT-TIP MARKERS

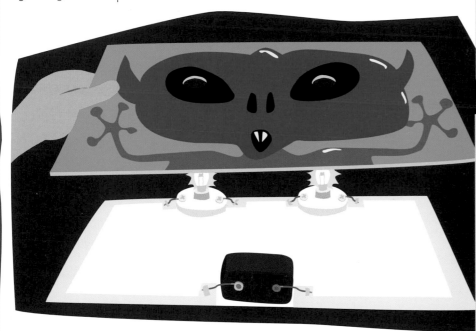

What's happening?
Because your circuit is so flat, you can stick it onto the back of a picture. To make your picture even more exciting, make a paper clip switch between the battery and the circuit board so you can turn your picture on and off (see page 11 for how to do this).

4 Using short lengths of real wire and some tape, connect the two bulbs and the battery to the foil strips. Do your light bulbs glow?

What's happening?
You have made a very flat circuit by replacing ordinary wires with strips of aluminum foil. The foil conducts electricity just like an ordinary wire, making the bulbs glow. The cardboard backing makes the circuit more durable and helps keep everything in place.

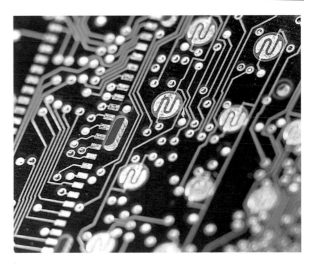

LOOK! NO WIRES
This printed circuit board comes from the inside of a TV remote control. Gadgets like this have very few ordinary wires—most of their circuits look like this. The wires of the circuit, stuck onto the backing, are about as thick as a layer of paint.

Branching out

A circuit doesn't have to be made in just one loop. Sometimes it's useful to give it two or more separate branches. When parts of a circuit are connected in the same loop, we say they are "in series." When they are in two separate loops, connected side by side, they are "in parallel." When bulbs are wired in parallel, it's easy to switch them on and off independently of one another.

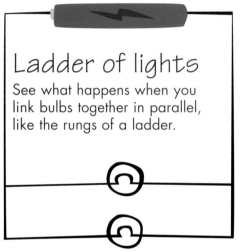

Ladder of lights

See what happens when you link bulbs together in parallel, like the rungs of a ladder.

YOU WILL NEED
15
- TWO SMALL FLASHLIGHT BULBS WITH A MAXIMUM VOLTAGE OF 4.5 VOLTS
- A 1.5-VOLT AA BATTERY
- TWO SHORT WIRES
- TWO LONG WIRES
- TAPE
- SCISSORS

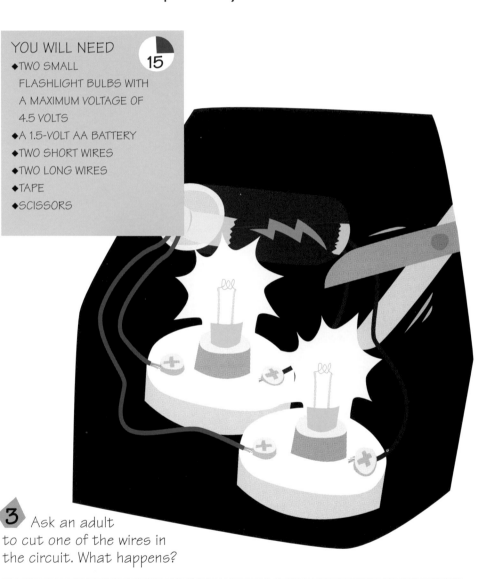

1 Follow the steps in "Bright idea" (page 10) to light up a bulb. Use short wires to connect the bulb to the battery. Make sure that the bulb is glowing.

3 Ask an adult to cut one of the wires in the circuit. What happens?

2 Using two slightly longer wires, connect another light bulb across the terminals of the battery. Do both light bulbs glow?

What's happening?
This circuit makes both bulbs glow brightly. That's because the two bulbs are wired in parallel—each bulb is in its own complete loop. Electricity can flow through both loops at the same time. It goes out of the battery, through the bulbs, then back into the battery again. When you cut a wire connecting one bulb to the battery, you turn that bulb off. However, you haven't broken the other bulb's loop, so that one continues glowing.

That's a switch

Follow steps 1 to 3 of "Ladder of lights" (left) to make a circuit that lights two bulbs in parallel. Now cut a wire connecting each bulb to the battery. Bridge the gap in each loop of your circuit with a paper clip switch (see page 11).

YOU WILL NEED

- TWO SMALL FLASHLIGHT BULBS WITH A MAXIMUM VOLTAGE OF 4.5 VOLTS
- A 1.5-VOLT AA BATTERY
- TWO SHORT WIRES
- TWO LONG WIRES
- TWO PAPER CLIPS
- TAPE

Can you use the paper clips to turn your lights on and off?

What's happening?

You can turn on either bulb, without affecting the other one, simply by pressing down the paper clip switch that's wired to that bulb. That's because the bulbs are wired in parallel. Each of the paper clip switches is wired in series with one of the bulbs.

FLASHBACK

First light

The first Christmas lights went on sale in the late 1800s. Unlike Christmas lights today, which are strung together in series, these were wired in parallel. This was important because the early bulbs frequently broke. When one bulb stopped working, the others kept on glowing.

NIGHT LIGHT

Towering over 40 stories high, this skyscraper is illuminated by thousands of lights that are connected in parallel. The lights on each floor make a different branch of a large parallel circuit. When security guards patrol the building at night, they can turn on one branch of the circuit at a time. This makes the lights glow on just one floor, saving electricity.

Feel the force

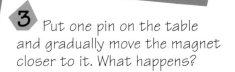

Magnets vary widely in size, shape, and strength, but they can all do two very special things—they can pull objects made of iron or nickel toward them, and they can attract or repel other magnets. Some magnets occur naturally. They have special magnetic properties as soon as they are mined from the ground. Others are made from nonmagnets, often using electricity. Materials like iron and nickel that are attracted toward a magnet are called magnetic materials.

Where do most of the pins stick to the magnet?

Jump to it!
Next time someone drops some pins, help pick them up with a magnet!

YOU WILL NEED
◆ A MAGNET
◆ STEEL PINS

5

2 Try to pick up a chain of pins with the magnet. How many pins can you pick up this way?

3 Put one pin on the table and gradually move the magnet closer to it. What happens?

1 Bring the magnet close to a small pile of loose pins. Can you pick up the pins with the magnet?

What's happening?
Pins stick to the magnet because they are made of steel, a material that contains a lot of iron. They are pulled toward it if they are nearby. The magnet's pull is strongest at its ends, so that is where most of the pins will stick. Scientists call the ends of the magnet its poles. When a pin sticks to the magnet, it becomes magnetized too, so it can pick up more pins itself. That's why you can pick up a chain of pins.

Is it magnetic?

You can find out which materials are magnetic by trying to pick up different objects around your home. (Warning: Magnets damage floppy disks, tapes, TVs, and computers, so keep them away from these!)

What's happening?

Only objects that contain iron or nickel are attracted to the magnet. You may have found these materials in some of the coins or keys that you tested. The magnet has no effect on objects like the wooden spoon and the pencil eraser because they don't contain any iron or nickel. This is also why the magnet has no effect on the soft drink can—it's made of aluminum.

Can sorter

You can use your magnet to sort steel and aluminum cans for recycling. Using the string and the tape, dangle the magnet from the bottom of a chair. Make sure the magnet is about 4 in. (10cm) above the ground. Roll your cans under the magnet one at a time. Do all the cans roll past the magnet smoothly?

What's happening?

The aluminum cans roll past the magnet, but the steel cans slow down. They may even stop moving altogether or stick to the magnet. This is because steel is a magnetic material. At recycling centers, cans are often sorted by moving them along a conveyor belt past a line of magnets.

HIGH FLYER

Tilting up and down to steer the plane, this airplane wing flap is controlled by a motor that uses a special magnet. Most magnets are mainly made of iron, but this one contains boron, a rare metal. This makes it much more powerful than an ordinary magnet. Only a tiny boron magnet is needed to move the wing flap. This keeps the wing as light as possible.

Pole to pole

Every magnet has two distinct poles. One pole is called "north," and one is called "south"—you can find out more about this on page 34. The area of force around a magnet is called its magnetic field.

Opposites attract

The forces between the poles of two magnets can be surprisingly strong—strong enough for you to feel them.

YOU WILL NEED
◆ A RULER
◆ A PENCIL
◆ TWO BAR MAGNETS
5

When do the forces between the magnets feel the strongest?

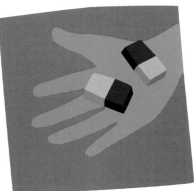

1 Take a close look at your two bar magnets. There should be paint marks on their ends to tell you which pole is which. They may be labeled "north" or "south," or they may simply be painted different colors.

2 Bring the two opposite poles of your two magnets close together. Can you feel the force that pulls them together?

3 Turn one of your magnets around so the two similar poles are facing each other. What force can you feel now? Hold the magnets 1 in. (2.5cm) apart, then 2 in. (5cm), then 3 in. (8cm). How close do the magnets have to be to make a force you can feel?

What's happening?

You feel a strong force between your two magnets when you bring them close together. When different poles are facing each other, this force attracts the magnets. When similar poles face each other, this force pushes them apart, or repels them. The force gets weaker as the magnets get farther apart.

Dancing feet

Put a magnet inside each sock and dangle the socks in the air. Move the socks close together and watch them dance around! Pad the socks out by wrapping each magnet in two layers of paper. Does the trick still work? Now put several layers of paper around the magnets. What happens?

How much paper can you put around the magnets before the trick stops working?

What's happening?

Unless your magnets are very weak, they will be able to attract or repel each other even when they are covered by your socks. A couple of layers of paper won't weaken the forces between them very much, but several layers of paper will. The stronger your magnets, the more paper you can wrap around them before the socks will stop dancing.

Spider stealth

Draw a spider about 2 in. (5cm) across and cut it out. Now tape a paper clip to the bottom of your spider and put it on the sheet of cardboard. You can make it move wherever you want using a magnet hidden underneath the cardboard!

What's happening?

If your magnet is strong enough, it will pull the paper clip toward it, even though it's separated from it by the cardboard. Anyone watching will see the spider move around in a most mysterious way!

ON THE RIGHT TRACK
A magnetic levitation (maglev) train never touches the rails below it. Magnetic forces between the track and runners on the bottom of the train make the train hover and move forward. It travels far more smoothly and quietly than an ordinary train.

Magnetic art

Magnets aren't only useful for making machines and tools. With a little imagination, you can also use them to create magnetic works of art! You can make interesting moving sculptures, like the one below, or fascinating, permanent pictures of a magnet's forces.

Peculiar pendulum

Three magnets will make this sculpture that swings in the strangest of ways.

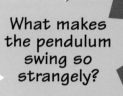

What makes the pendulum swing so strangely?

YOU WILL NEED
◆ THREE MAGNETS
10
◆ AN IRON NAIL
◆ STRING
◆ A CHAIR
◆ MODELING CLAY
◆ TAPE

1 Tie some string to the head of your nail, then dangle the nail under the chair. Make sure one of your magnets can fit underneath your hanging nail with a gap of about 1/3 in. (1cm).

2 Tap the nail gently and watch it swing back and forth like a pendulum. Make sure there are no magnets near your nail when you do this.

3 Use some modeling clay to attach the three magnets to the floor, as shown. Make sure the like poles of the magnets are facing each other. The poles should be about 3/4 in. (2cm) apart.

4 Move the chair so the nail is directly over the center of the group of magnets. Gently tap the nail again. What happens?

What's happening?
When there are no magnets around, the nail swings back and forth smoothly, like the pendulum of an old-fashioned clock. The only force the nail feels is the force of gravity. When you put the magnets beneath the nail, it swings in a crazy, unpredictable manner. This is because it also feels a force from each of the magnets. As it swings nearer to and farther from each magnet, the force on it varies continually.

Get the picture

Place the magnet under a sheet of paper and sprinkle iron filings onto the paper. The filings will form a definite pattern. Put a little paint on the toothbrush, then flick the toothbrush with your finger to spray paint onto the paper. When the paint is dry, carefully remove the magnet and filings.

Where do most of the filings settle?

What's happening?

Most filings settle around the poles, because this is where the force of the magnet is greatest. Others settle in onion-shaped rings around the magnet. These rings are called lines of force. The pattern of the filings is perfectly symmetrical because the magnet creates exactly the same force at each pole and on each side.

FLASHBACK

Flea circus

Some tricksters in the 1800s pretended they had performing fleas. They would entertain people with their flea circuses at theaters and fairgrounds. The tricksters pulled strings and moved tiny metal props with hidden magnets to make it look like the circus contained a team of flea acrobats.

NO STRINGS ATTACHED

Most parts of a puppet are controlled by strings, but this puppet's lips are controlled by a pair of magnets. Its mouth is normally held closed by a spring, but when the magnets are activated, they create a force that pushes its lips apart so it can "speak."

Make your own magnets

Every magnet is made of billions of tiny magnets, called domains, that are all lined up in the same direction. Other materials have domains too, but theirs are all jumbled up. If you have a magnet, you can tease the domains of magnetic materials to make them face the same way. This turns the materials into new magnets.

Make a magnet

To turn a paper clip into a magnet, you just have to stroke it the right way.

YOU WILL NEED
◆ TWO STEEL PAPER CLIPS
◆ A MAGNET
◆ MODELING CLAY

10

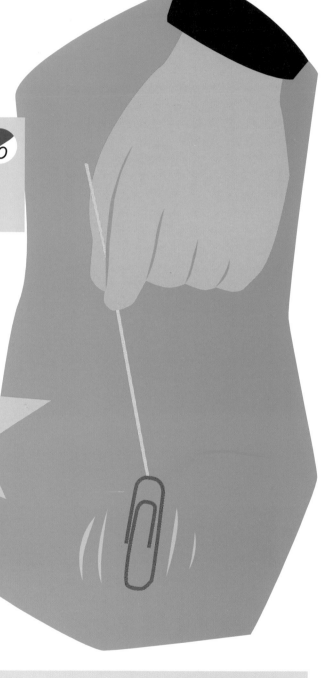

1 Open out one steel paper clip into a straight line and lay it on a firm surface. Keep it in place with some modeling clay.

What makes the paper clip turn into a magnet?

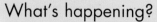

3 Move the bar magnet out of the way, pick up your steel paper clip, and test it. Can you pick up another paper clip with it?

2 Holding the bar magnet in one hand, move it through the air in a loop like this, close to the paper clip. Repeat this several times. Take care to keep the magnet facing the same way. Do not change the direction of the loop.

What's happening?

When you stroke the steel paper clip with a magnet, you turn the paper clip into a magnet too, or magnetize it. This is because the magnet pulls at the domains of the paper clip until they all face in one direction. The magnet can move the domains around because the domains themselves are microscopic magnets.

Magnetic mobile

Make a magnetic mobile and see how long it lasts. Follow the steps in "Make a magnet" (left) to magnetize your metal objects. Suspend your largest object from a piece of string just above floor level, then link together as many of the other objects as you can. Be careful with the nails! Keep the items together using the magnetic forces between them—don't use tape or glue. Check your mobile to see what happens.

How long does your mobile last?

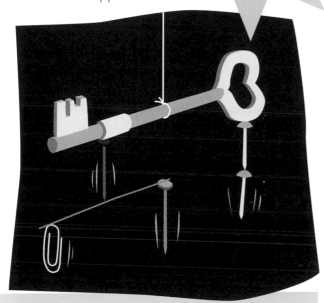

What's happening?

Since every part of this mobile is a magnet, you can keep it together without glue or tape. Over time, though, the magnetism of your objects will fade. This happens faster if the mobile gets knocked or dropped. Every small shock to the mobile jumbles up its domains a little. This reduces its magnetism. Steel objects stay magnetic far longer than iron objects, because their domains are harder to jumble.

Off the menu

Hundreds of years ago, onions and garlic were banned from many ships' rations. Ships navigated using magnetic compasses (see page 34), and crews mistakenly believed that onions and garlic affected magnets! The sailors worried that they would lose their way if the ship's compasses became confused.

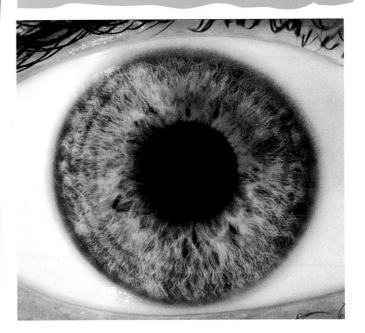

EYE FULL

Magnets can be used to safely remove some metal objects from the eye. The metal can be removed without touching the eye, so the eye is far less likely to be damaged. Surgeons usually magnify their view of an eye before they perform the delicate task of pulling an object from it.

Mini-magnets

You can't destroy a magnet just by chopping it in half. Both halves of the magnet will still have billions of domains that all point in the same direction. These domains will give both halves their magnetism.

Double up

Ask an adult to help you chop a homemade magnet in half—you'll have two homemade mini-magnets!

1 Follow the instructions in "Make a magnet" (page 30) to turn a paper clip into a homemade magnet. Check that the homemade magnet works.

How does cutting a magnet in half make two magnets?

4 Now dangle one half of the broken magnet from another piece of thread. Hold the other half close to it. Can you make the two halves attract each other? What happens if you turn around the half of the magnet that's in your hand?

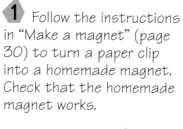

2 Ask an adult to chop the homemade magnet in half, using wire clippers or pliers.

3 Dangle an ordinary metal paper clip from a piece of thread. Hold one half of the broken homemade magnet close to it. Does it attract the paper clip? Repeat this step using the other half of the homemade magnet.

What's happening?

When you chopped the homemade magnet in half, you made two mini-magnets. That's because each half still has a large number of domains all facing in the same direction. Each mini-magnet can attract a paper clip. Since it has a north and a south pole, it can also attract and repel the other mini-magnet. You can cut the homemade magnet into more pieces to make even smaller magnets.

Wipe out

Play an unwanted audiocassette and stop it about halfway through. Take the cassette out of the cassette player and pull out a loop of tape about 12 in. (30cm) long. Pass a magnet close to the end of the loop of tape. Be careful not to bring it close to the rest of the tape. Carefully wind the loop back into the cassette, then play it again. What happens when you reach the part of the tape that was near the magnet?

YOU WILL NEED 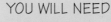 10
◆ AN UNWANTED AUDIOCASSETTE WITH MUSIC RECORDED ON IT (ASK PERMISSION FIRST!)
◆ A CASSETTE PLAYER
◆ A MAGNET

What's happening?

The magnet erased the sound from part of the tape. Small groups of magnetic granules on the tape store tiny fragments of sound. Each fragment is less than one ten-thousandth of a second long. The granules have stronger magnetism when a louder sound is stored. When you pass a magnet close to the tape, you overpower the magnetism of each group of granules, wiping out this stored information.

FLASHBACK

Sounds dangerous

Playing some of the first magnetic recordings, in the 1930s, was a dangerous business. Instead of using magnetic granules on tape, people stored sound on a piece of magnetized wire. To play back the sound, the wire had to move through a machine at high speed. If the wire snapped, it could break loose, cutting through anything—or anyone—in its path. Listeners had to be ready to make a quick getaway!

COMPUTER HARD DISK
The hard disk in your computer uses magnetism to store words, pictures, and other information. Tiny magnets change the pattern of the magnetism to store information or to erase it.

Map it out

Ever since people discovered magnets, they have used them to find their way from place to place. Magnets can be used to navigate because they always turn to face north. This is because they are affected by the earth, which itself acts like a very big, but weak, magnet. A magnet used to find north is called a compass.

Traveling light

This compass, which can fit in a matchbox, is also light enough to float on water.

YOU WILL NEED
- A MAGNET
- A STEEL PIN
- A CORK
- MODELING CLAY
- A LARGE PLASTIC BOWL
- WATER
- A SHARP KNIFE (ASK AN ADULT)

15

1 Following the instructions in "Make a magnet" (page 30), use the magnet to magnetize the steel pin.

2 Ask an adult to cut a small disk, about ½ in. (1.25cm) thick, from the end of the cork, using the knife. Attach the pin to the top of the cork with a tiny amount of modeling clay.

3 Fill the bowl with water. Then carefully float the steel pin and cork in it.

What happens to the pin when you turn the bowl?

Stone followers

Magnetite, a type of iron, is a naturally occurring magnet. Tiny fragments of magnetite are often called lodestones, meaning "leading stones," because they can be used to point north, leading the way home. The Chinese were the first to discover that lodestones could be used to navigate. They used lodestones to make the first compasses about 3,000 years ago.

34

About-turn

You can confuse your compass. Follow the steps in "Traveling light" (left) to make a floating compass. Make sure it points in a north–south direction when it settles. Then bring a magnet an inch or so away from your compass. What happens?

Does your compass always point north?

YOU WILL NEED
20
◆ A MAGNET
◆ THE ITEMS USED IN "TRAVELING LIGHT" (LEFT)

What's happening?

As soon as you bring a magnet close to your compass, the compass' poles spin toward the magnet's poles, so the compass stops pointing north. That's because your magnet is much stronger than the earth's magnetism. The magnet overpowers the earth's magnetism, confusing the compass.

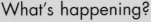

4 Wait for the steel pin and cork to stop turning. Draw a picture of the pin on a piece of paper and lay it beside the bowl to remind you which way the needle faces.

What's happening?

When it stops turning, the magnetized steel pin will always point in the same direction, even if you turn the bowl. That direction is roughly north–south. It does this because its north and south poles align with the magnetic poles of the earth, which itself is a giant, weak magnet. One pole of the earth's magnetism is roughly north on the map. The other is roughly south.

FLY AWAY HOME
With an amazing sense of direction, pigeons like these can find their way home even after they are moved hundreds of miles away. Scientists think homing pigeons are good navigators partly because they can sense the earth's magnetism.

Pick-up power

Electricity and magnetism are very closely linked. When electricity flows through a wire, it turns the wire into a magnet—though it is usually too weak to pick anything up. When you move a magnet close to a wire, you make a tiny current. Our homes are full of machines that use this connection between electricity and magnetism. We call the connection electromagnetism.

Electric magnet

Send electricity through a coil of wire to make a strong magnet. The wires in this experiment could get warm—ask an adult for help.

YOU WILL NEED
- A VERY LONG INSULATED WIRE
- AN IRON NAIL
- A PAPER CLIP
- A 9-VOLT BATTERY
- TAPE
- STEEL PINS

15

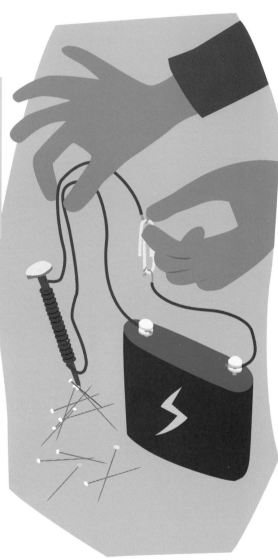

How can an iron nail be turned into a magnet?

1 Wind the wire tightly around the iron nail at least ten times, holding it in place with tape.

2 Connect one end of the wire to a terminal of your battery. Connect the other end to the other terminal, and add a paper clip switch (see page 11).

3 Hold the nail over a pile of steel pins as you press down the switch to turn on the circuit. What happens? Let go of the switch to turn the circuit off. What happens now?

What's happening?
When you press the switch down, the iron nail picks up pins. That's because electricity flows through the circuit, turning its wires into weak magnets. The magnetism is concentrated when the wire is coiled. It makes a magnetic force strong enough to turn the nail into a magnet. A magnet like this, which only works when electricity flows around it, is called an electromagnet.

Electric eels

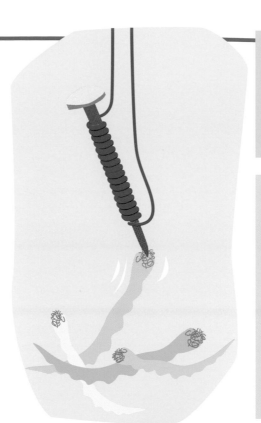

Follow the steps in "Electric magnet" (left) to make an electromagnet. Then use it to challenge a friend to a game of electric eels. Cut out some eels from tissue paper and stick tiny pieces of steel wool to their heads. Take turns picking up eels, against the clock, using the electromagnet. If you pick up one eel, you can keep it. If you pick up two or more, you have to throw them back! You'll have to use all your skill to turn the electromagnet on and off at the right time.

What's happening?

The steel wool on the eels' heads is attracted by the electromagnet, so you can use it to pick the eels up. But the nail is magnetized only when the paper clip switch is on. When the switch is off, there is no electric current running through the circuit, so there is no magnetism.

FLASHBACK

Moving idea

It's surprising to know that when scientist Michael Faraday demonstrated the first motor in 1821, he had trouble convincing people that electromagnetism would be useful. Today the link between electricity and magnetism enables us to build all kinds of machines that use electricity to control how things move. An electric motor and a vibrating speaker are just a few examples.

DOWN IN THE DUMPS
Dumps and junkyards often have huge cranes that carry electromagnets, like this one. They are strong enough to pick up huge hunks of metal—even whole cars.

Glossary

Attract Two things attract each other if they try to pull closer together. This happens when they have opposite electrical charges (when one has too many electrons and the other has too few). A magnet will attract objects that contain a lot of iron or nickel. Two magnets will attract each other if the north pole of one is close to the south pole of the other.

Charge Something has a charge if it has too many or too few electrons. This could happen because it has been rubbed with another object to make static electricity. Two objects have the same type of charge if they've both lost electrons or if they've both gained them. They have opposite charges if one has gained electrons but the other has lost them.

Compass A device that can be used to find out which way is north. The most important part of a compass is the needle, which is a magnet. Like all magnets, the needle will point in a roughly north–south direction when left to swing freely.

Conductor A substance that electricity can flow through easily. Metal and water are both good conductors. These are the raw materials of many electrical devices, such as wires, switches, and light bulbs. The word "conductor" is also used to talk about things besides electricity. For instance, engineers often ask if a material is a good conductor of heat.

Current A measure of how much electricity is flowing. Current is measured in amperes (A). The more easily a battery can push electricity around a circuit, the larger the current. A larger current means more electrons are flowing through the circuit.

Domains The millions of mini-magnets, too small to see, that make up every material. The domains of a magnet all face in the same direction. Its magnetism will fade if its domains get jumbled (for example, if it is hit with a hammer.)

Electricity The form of energy that makes house lights, televisions, and all other electrical things work. Electricity is created by particles called electrons, which are far too tiny to see. Electrons make current electricity when they flow through things like wires and light bulbs. When they are not moving, electrons make static electricity.

Electromagnet A magnet that only works when electricity flows through it. Most electromagnets are made of a coil of wire wrapped around metal to boost its magnetic strength.

Electron A particle that is far too tiny to see. There are one or more electrons in every atom. When electrons flow through things, such as a wire, they make current electricity. When they rub off of one thing and onto another, they make static electricity.

Energy The ability to do work. Heat and electricity are two types of energy.

Filament The thin, coiled wire inside a light bulb that makes the bulb glow. It is hard for electricity to flow through this wire, so it turns into another form of energy—heat. This makes the filament glow white hot, producing light.

Insulator A substance that electricity cannot flow through easily. Wood, paper, glass, and plastic are all good insulators. Electric machines and parts are often covered in insulators to make them safe—for example, wires are often covered in plastic, and a television is built inside a plastic box. The word "insulator" is also used to talk about other forms of energy. For instance, a material may be a good insulator of heat.

Magnet An object that can pull iron or nickel objects toward it. Magnets can also attract or repel other magnets. Some rocks, like magnetite, are naturally occuring magnets. Other magnets can be made in the laboratory—for instance, by stroking iron or nickel with other magnets.

Magnetic field The area around a magnet where it can noticeably attract or repel things. Stronger magnets have a larger magnetic field.

Magnetic materials Materials that are attracted toward magnets. Iron and nickel are magnetic materials. So are many materials that contain either of these two metals. Steel, for example, contains a lot of iron, so it is a magnetic material.

Parallel The word used to describe electrical parts that have been wired into two or more separate loops. Each loop lets electricity flow out of the battery, through itself, then back into the battery again.

Poles The two areas of a magnet, usually at its ends, in which the magnet's pull is strongest. If you let a magnet swing freely, one pole will always end up pointing approximately south. This pole is the magnet's south pole. The other, called the magnet's north pole, will always end up pointing roughly north. The poles end up pointing in these directions because they are attracted to the north and south poles of the earth, which is itself a giant magnet.

Repel Two things repel each other if they try to push away from each other. This happens when they have the same type of electrical charge (when both objects have too few electrons or both have too many). Two magnets will repel each other if the north pole of one is close to the north pole of the other. They will also repel if their south poles are close together.

Series The word used to describe electrical things that have been strung together in a single loop. This loop lets electricity flow out of the battery, through each part in the loop, then into the battery again.

Short circuit A very easy path that electricity can take around a circuit. A wire connected directly to the two terminals of a battery will make a short circuit. Electricity will always take a short circuit when it can.

Static electricity A type of electricity made by rubbing certain things together, such as a nylon cloth and a plastic ruler. When you do this, you brush electrons off of one item and onto the other. This gives both objects an electrical charge.

Voltage A measure of the electrical "push" a battery can give to the electrons flowing around a circuit. This push is measured in volts (V). A 4.5-volt battery, for example, has three times the electrical push of a 1.5-volt battery. Most batteries have their voltage written on their casing.

Index

Photography Credits

London Features International 29

Science Photo Library
21, 33

Pictor International 15

PowerStock Photo Library 37

Telegraph Colour Library 11, 25

Tony Stone 13, 19, 23, 31, 35

Corbis 7, 9

Central Japan Railway Company
27

Royal National Lifeboat Institution
17